D1115985

Farmer Johnson's Psycho Dairy Farm

For Environmentally Aware Barnyard Animals

by

Steve Phillips

A DELL TRADE PAPERBACK

Published by
Dell Publishing
a division of
Bantam Doubleday Dell Publishing Group, Inc.
666 Fifth Avenue
New York, New York 10103

Library of Congress Cataloging in Publication Data

Phillips, Steve, 1953–
    Farmer Johnson's psycho dairy farm for environmentally aware
barnyard animals / Steve Phillips.
        p.   cm.
    ISBN 0-440-50509-7 : $8.00
    1. Environmental psychology—Caricatures and cartoons.
2. American wit and humor, Pictorial. I. Title.
NC1429.P57A4   1992
741.5'973—dc20   91-32619
                                                          CIP

Printed in the United States of America

Published simultaneously in Canada

November 1992

10   9   8   7   6   5   4   3   2   1

FFG

TO OPEN

SHAKE BEFORE SERVING

SELL BY

PUSH UP HERE

LOW FAT

LACTOSE-REDUCED

An ULTRA-Pasturized

THANKYOU!

Without the love & Friendship of the following people, this book would be nothing but a mere meadow muffin
~ steve

Freckles of Love, Ma, Shmenkin, Farticus, My LE LE LE dee dee deeee, TRAV-LiNKus, Patti, That EMILY-babe, MISTER Dolan (HIS BEST Friend in-the-whole-wide-world-since-Kindergarten), RAM-Zilla, Wendalah, DRUNK-mAN, TOM the NAP-MAN, DENI-WENi, KEV-O, The REGULARS at STEVE MCGRAWS, Harriet and "Da Group", Lil Kaitland, Tom Chalmers & Pam Woodruff, TIM Forker—who started it all, Betty-YAMS, Lawrence Kelly-author, whose PLAY "OUT" appears nightly on a placemat at Steve McGraws, Special thanks to Jennifer Dale & the Summer of '90, Don Shimoda, Owen Meany, and to the child in all of us.

KEEP REFRIGERATED

ONE QUART (946 mL)

Daisy

" Is there more to life
than just milking and
grazing?"

Elrod

"Toxic dumping, banking scandals,
oil spills...
and they call **ME** a swine !!"

Bubbles

" I ask myself,
why am I here?
where am I going?"

Farmer Johnson

"I ask myself, Why am I here, and where are MY EGGS!?"

and
SPECIAL
Guest Star...

Burt
the AMAZING Invisible Bull!

Daisy wonders, "Is there more to life than just milking and grazing?"

While at the supermarket, Elrod recognizes his long-lost pal, Fred

Daisy, Bubbles and Elrod suspect that someone is slipping "SUPER HORMONES" in their feed

Daisy practices creative visualization

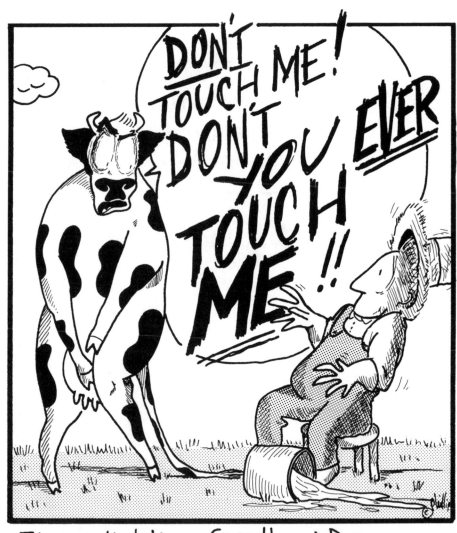

It was that time of month, and Daisy was suffering from "PRE MILKING SYNDROME!"

Farmer Johnson grows impatient waiting for Daisy to finish up her morning *t'ai chi*

Bubbles practices
creative visualization

"COW" by Robert MOOplethorpe

Farmer Johnson shrinks his cows in a mad plot to become the **KING** of **CONDENSED MILK**!

It was true what they said...
Farmer Johnson was "cow-dependent"

Fearing current diet trends would discourage sales of beef and pork, Farmer Johnson comes up with a brilliant idea!

PART PIG
PART MACHINE
ALL CHOP...

ROBO CHOP

THE LOIN ENFORCEMENT CYPORK OF THE FUTURE

Farmer Johnson begins to suspect that the acid rain showers are indeed affecting his dairy products

Bubbles the Chicken catches up on the latest barnyard best seller

THESE ARE YOUR EGGS...

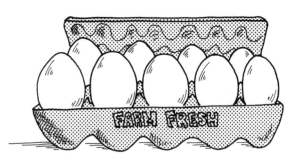

THESE ARE YOUR EGGS ON DRUGS

Barnyard Bickering

Although they hadn't seen each other in a while, Elrod felt Dora's summer with the **NFL** had changed her somehow

While practicing his mime routine, Elrod accidentally gets trapped in his "Invisible box

Farmer Johnson was pleased to discover that Daisy's acupuncture treatments not only helped his cable reception...

... but enabled him to get HBO-FREE!!

Cow Tipping

Pigcasso

Farmer Johnson suspects his animals are secretly being used for cosmetic testing

Elrod watches his favorite syndicated TV show,
"The Honey Mooers"

and once again, no one listened to Chicken Little

Up until now, no one had suspected Elrod of...

It's what Farmer Johnson
hated most...
The **LEVITATING CHICKENS!**

Daisy has another
"out-of-barnyard"
experience

Elrod, Daisy and Bubbles couldn't deny it any longer—
the Sixties were back!

COWS of the 50s

cows of the 60s

COWS of the 70s

©Phillips

COWS of the 80s

© Phillips

Cows of the 90s

While "channeling" the spirit of Elsie the Cow
Daisy accidentally contacts "Mr. Ed"

As the temperature rose to a blistering 105°, Farmer Johnson soon discovered that his **hematite** healing crystal was actually one of Daisy's cow chips

Farmer Johnson suspects that Daisy is having
another mid-life crisis

Farmer Johnson suspects Daisy's constant questioning may be affecting his sale of beef

Daisy explains that although she's very fond
of Duke they just aren't astrologically compatible

Elrod knew Cousin Porky would end up like this
for he had warned him countless times of the
dangers of smoking in bed

Once again Farmer Johnson had
to delay the nightly milking
while Daisy finished up her
evening aerobics

...and once again Farmer Johnson had to rescue Daisy from her evening aerobics

Farmer Johnson grew weary
of Daisy's psychic spoon-bending
tricks

He wasn't sure, but something told
Farmer Johnson that the local Nuclear
Power Plant was leaking again

Farmer Johnson suspects his animals are possessed by the ghost of Elvis

Farmer Johnson was pleased that the use of genetically engineered hormones produced BIGGER barnyard animals, resulting in BIGGER profits!

It also resulted in BIGGER cow pies

Farmer Johnson had TWO options:
ONE — agree with Bubbles' philosophy of "Low Egg Productivity," OR
TWO — choke her scrawny little neck

THE DAILY UDDER

REV. PIGGY SWAGGERT CAUGHT WALLOWING IN MUD WITH A COUPLE OF CHICKS

PENNSYLVANIA – "I'M INNOCENT!" claimed renowned evangelist Piggy Swaggert after local religious leaders found the popular minister cavorting with two chicks of the evening.

"I was just trying to show them the evils of their ways and besides, I needed the eggs!"

However, religious leaders have long felt the flamboyant leader has been secretly living a life of "sin."

"If others want to start Mud slinging, well, I'm ready!" said Rev. Piggy.

MORE ON PAGE 7

© Phillips

(UPI) LOCAL RELIGIOUS LEADERS EXPOSE THE SCANDAL

FIGURE A-1

With your hoofs and hind legs **firmly** on the ground, inhale and gradually **push** the grass away, straightening your **front** legs and unfolding your hind legs. Excellent for **milk retention** and relieving cramping udders

FIGURE A-2

Lower your belly to the ground. **Gently** move your udders to the side to avoid **painful** squashing. Straighten **front** legs and stretch your hind legs until they rest on the ground. **Wonderful** for those days when you **know** you'll be on **your hoofs** for hours!

MORE SCENES FROM... Daisy the Cow's UDDER WORKOUT Video

FIGURE A-3

With knees bent, let your spine **hang** between your thighs. **Feel** the weight drop through the spine and out through the **head**. An excellent **postmilking position** and great for spotting annoying **flies**

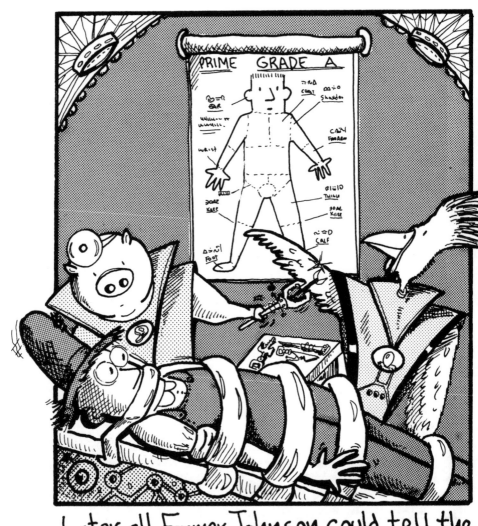

Later, all Farmer Johnson could tell the FBI was that his alien kidnappers smelled like bacon and eggs

Determined to be kosher, Elrod visits his pal from the "old neighborhood" – Roger Rabbi

Daisy learns about coping with
on-the-job stress

Farmer Johnson appreciated Bubbles' Zen philosophy,
but at 4am all he could think was
"SHUT UP and LAY EGGS!!"

While playing the Windham Hill version of "Old MacDonald" backward at slow speed, Elrod discovers its secret "Satanic" Message!

To Farmer Johnson's delight, Daisy
momentarily reverts back to her
past life as...

"...Selma, the Chicken Queen"

Farmer Johnson rethinks the whole
"free range" chicken thing

FARMER Johnson's KNOW YOUR FOOD QUIZ #1

Q. WOULD YOU still find these foods appetizing if they had MORE descriptive names?

Ⓐ EGGS

ONE DOZEN

OR
"things that come from a chicken's behind"

Ⓑ LETTUCE

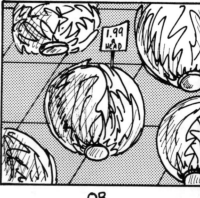

1.99 A HEAD

OR
"crunchy green stuff that rabbits pee on"

If you add a dash of balsamic vinegar and tamari, it cuts that "toxic-dump" aftertaste
©Phillips

The greenhouse effect was definitely taking it's toll on Farmer Johnson's pigs and chickens

Farmer Johnson prepares his chickens
for market

Farmer Johnson had that certain...
ohhh, shall we say... animal magnetism?

It was as if the Cable reception of every TV set in America had **MAGICALLY** cleared up!
No one knew why. No one but **ELROD!!**

Television Repairmen
from
PLANET X

Quack addicts

Elrod accidentally Knocks Farmer Johnson's minoxidil into the cheese maker, creating a revolutionary new dairy/grooming product— "CHEEZE-WIGS!"

Barnyard identity crisis

Farmer Johnson yearned for the good ol' da
when life was simple and all a pig did wa
wallow in mud

Suddenly Farmer Johnson realizes he's **NOT** milking **ELSA**, "the Amazing Invisible Cow," but rather...

...**BURT**, "the Amazing Invisible Bull"

At the age of four, Steve watched his father perform in Broadway musicals from a backstage vantage point. From then on, he was never satisfied with looking at life from obvious angles.

This outlook carried on as Steve tackled such diverse occupations as bartender, television producer, charity fund-raiser, and special events director for an organization benefiting the mentally handicapped. Unbeknownst to him, he was gathering many of the experiences that would appear in his cards, calendars, and books that strike a funny and familiar chord.

It was while bartending that Steve was struck by the idea of affectionately exposing the day-to-day tribulations that his customers so often expressed. What has ensued is a humorous look at some of life's most perplexing conditions and problems—dieting, mid-life crisis, PMS, pregnancy, and stress. Through his unique perspective, Steve reminds us that most of our problems are not life-threatening, and could certainly use a good laugh!

Steve continues to explore and capture the curiosity of people being themselves. Though residing in New York City, a place filled with the complexity of living, he still tries to maintain the demeanor of an innocent observer, like a child lying in his crib trying to see the mystery beyond his bottle. Look for some of Steve's other work on recycled paper greeting cards and calendars and Landmark calendars.